LORD
of the
evening

by FRANK TOPPING

Illustrations by Noeline Kelly

LUTTERWORTH PRESS
Guildford and London

First published in Great Britain 1979
Second impression 1981

By the same author
LORD OF THE MORNING

These prayers are dedicated
To those unseen friends, the radio listeners, who have
encouraged me with their letters;
To my wife, JUNE, who has been patient with my late
night scribbling;
To my children, ANNE, SIMON and MARK, who have
inspired many of these meditations, but especially to
ANNE, who typed all of them.

ISBN 0 7188 2417 2

Set in 12/14 pt Optima

Printed in Great Britain by
Ebenezer Baylis & Son Limited
The Trinity Press, Worcester and London

CONTENTS

MAY EVERY DAY   5

PATIENCE   6

STARS   9

BEDTIME   11

MISTAKES   14

LOOKING FOR PEACE   16

SLEEP ON IT   19

THE GIFT OF VISION   21

FACING THE TRUTH   24

A SMILE   26

THE EMPTY HOUSE   29

I AM NOT WORTHY   31

COMFORT THE SORROWFUL   34

MASKS   37

ALL MY TOMORROWS   40

SONS AND DAUGHTERS   42

I'M SORRY   45

EYES TO SEE   47

A QUIET MIND   50

THE CHILD AND THE FATHER   52

COURAGE FOR THE NIGHT   55

THE HOPE OF HIS COMING   57

BEFORE I SLEEP   61

CHRISTMAS EVE   65

THE INSTRUMENTS OF PEACE   68

THE LANGUAGE OF PRAYER   73

May every day
Begin with space
Enough to see
My saviour's face.

May every hour
Possess within it
The space to live
A prayerful minute.

And may I find,
From night's alarms,
The space between
My saviour's arms.

Aylesford Priory Retreat

PATIENCE

I wish I had more patience
I'm always wanting things, now,
Wishing for things to happen now.
It isn't easy to be patient
When every day I pass a huge poster
Saying 'Why wait? Buy it now!'
I suppose I live in a society
That demands *instant* satisfaction.
'Have it today' with easy payments, credit cards
And hire purchase.
But I can't blame society.
Society is me and my friends.

When I was a child
Part of the spice of life was waiting for things.
Waiting for a bike, a watch,
Waiting for Saturday, when at last
I had saved enough pocket money
To buy that penknife.

Waiting was a pleasure that could be savoured.
Now, waiting is an irritation.
My patience is short
When things don't happen soon enough.
I even expect my prayers to be answered *instantly*.

Lord help me to be patient
Not only in wanting things
But help me to be patient with people.
Help me to be patient with my wife and children.
Each day, each hour, each minute,
Help me to breathe slowly, to listen and to wait.
Help me to be patient with myself,
And not least, to wait patiently for your guidance
This night and always.

STARS

Tonight the sky is calm
With the still, cool light of stars,
And yet they are not silent.
On such a night
The heavens salute their creator
With shouts of joy
Too exquisite for the human ear.
Tonight is a festival.
Virtuoso performers take their places
Form dazzling patterns
Brilliant clusters
And they are perfect.

And I have known them
These stars
From the days of my childhood
To the days of my children.
Walking down country lanes
We have identified the Plough
Pointed to the Pole
And felt small beneath their majesty.

On such a night I have held the North Star
Between the mainmast shrouds of a tall ship
Steering for home.
Ageless mariners have looked
To that constant star
And are looking, tonight.

Tonight, each star and planet
Is the splash of a sounding
Measuring the depth of the Almighty.
Tonight there is so much laughter in the sky
Because you have filled it with old friends
Holding lanterns
And singing songs of love across the heavens.
And once again I know
That your light is ever before me.

BEDTIME

In this evening hour
In the last minutes
Of a long day
I am grateful for the joy
Of clean sheets and a pillow,
For the prospect
Of seven or eight hours
Of physical rest,
For the pleasure of closing my eyes.
Lord of the evening
Thank you for the night,
For my bed
And for sleep.

So often bedtime is simply a gap
Between days.
A habit, a necessary interruption
When really
It is yet another gift
That I take for granted.
To lie in bed is luxury.
Here, between the sheets,
Beneath my eyelids
The trials of today
Sink into my subconscious
And become history.

Lord of the night
Thank you for the rest
That each sunset brings,
For the peace and quietness
Of late hours,
For the stillness
Of the stars and the night.
And may those who cannot sleep
Know the comfort of your presence.

Lord help me to enjoy
The gift of evening,
Let me not relive the tensions
Of the day that has gone;
Prevent me from fighting tomorrow's battles
Before tomorrow's dawn.
Let me savour this space.
Let me be conscious of these untroubled
Minutes and seconds.
Let me be refreshed.
Let me rest mind and body.
Let me place my trust
In you, who have led me
To this time and place,
In you, the giver of life and light
And sleep.

MISTAKES

Lord of the evening
Someone let me down today.
I was upset and said harsh things.
It's so easy to be superior
When other people make mistakes,
To wag the finger, shake the head,
As if I had never made a mistake,
Never let anyone down.
And if I concede that there are times
When I am less than perfect,
I expect other people to be understanding
To be sympathetic, kind, merciful.

Lord of the evening
Forgive me
For my lack of understanding.

Lord, when I have made mistakes
I hope that they will soon be forgotten,
That people will behave
As if they never happened.
I don't want to feel the flush of guilt
That comes whenever my errors
Are brought into the open.
Yet so often I am less than kind
To those who have offended me.

Lord, help me to show the same mercy to others
That I would wish for myself.
Lord, preserve me
From any desire for revenge.
Stop me from ever trying
To get my own back.
You taught hard lessons
When you told us to 'turn the other cheek',
'Love your enemies', 'go the extra mile'.
So often I have been your enemy
Because of my unkindness
My selfishness
My lack of love.
Yet I know that you still love me,
That there is no end to your mercy.
Loving, patient, suffering Lord,
Help me to give to others
The forgiving love I continually receive from you.

LOOKING FOR PEACE

In quietness I sometimes realise
How much I need noise.
In quietness I sometimes see
The peace that belongs
To a lively household
Full of people.
So often
I've searched for peace
Longed for peace
And in my search confused 'peace'
With being alone or being still.
Finding quietness and tranquility
Is easy, they are just places,
But peace is in the mind.

So I ask myself, what are
The moments of real peace of mind
That I have known,
And I find that I have been at peace
In laughter, in real genuine laughter.
And laughter shared is even better.
At mealtimes
In conversation with friends round a table
There are moments of mutual peace.
Life is not so difficult
When you talk about it
With a knife and a fork in your hand.

And work
In work there can be peace,
Problems recede, even disappear
In the concentration
Of doing some job well.

In prayer
When I view my problems
Held up in relief against eternity
Peace begins.
In prayer
When I realise that there is no need
For words
There is the peace
That passes my understanding.

I have looked to distant dreams
For peace,
But your peace
Is in the commonplace
In the daily round.
Lord help me to find and enjoy
The peace that lives
In laughter
In conversation
In friendship
In family
In work
And in prayer.

Lord of the evening
May I always remember
That the knowledge of your love
Is the touch of peace
And that nothing is beyond your reach.

SLEEP ON IT

Here I am
At the end of another day
With so many things I should have done,
Not done.
There are letters I should have written
People I should have talked to
Work I should have started
And work I should have finished.
Unanswered family questions
About the children
Their progress at school
Their choice of career.
Personal questions
Where do I stand?
What is my next step?
And suddenly night has fallen
And the streets are still.

But what am I asking?
It would be a strange day
In which all work was finished.
All questions answered
All decisions made.
There wouldn't be much to live for.

To be alive
Is to work
To make efforts
To ask questions.
Living needs contrasts, opposites.
If there is no work there is no rest.
Without questions there are no answers.
All laughter and no tears
Would be nonsense.
Failure enriches success.
Why should I think that this day
Has been any less fulfilled than others?
Every day is incomplete,
Every day leaves something for tomorrow,
That's what tomorrow is for.

Lord of the night
Be with me through the hours of darkness,
Let all my questions,
Problems, decisions,
Be enveloped in sleep
That through the mystery
Of the sleeping mind
The difficulties of this day
Will be seen to be easier
In the morning light.
Into your hands O Lord,
I commit my spirit.

THE GIFT OF VISION

Lord, in these few moments
Before sleep
I wish there was more time
To think things over.
But how long do I need
When it only takes a few seconds
To travel a long way in thought?
In a few seconds
I can recapture the peace
That has been stored in my mind
Over years.
In the twinkle of an eye
I can see mountains and lakes,
Sanctuaries of peace in my head.

Even in the bustle
Of my everyday work
It is possible to retreat
For a brief instant
To the peace that I have known
And that still exists.

Lord you have given us
The gift of vision,
The ability to look beyond
The difficulties that surround us,
Help me to use that vision
To be able to stand back
From immediate problems
To see them against the immensity of time.
For against a vision like that
My problems begin to look small.

Lord of life
Help me to recognise the moments
That are given to me each day,
Moments of stillness
That can bring me into your presence,
Moments that glimpse eternity
Through the flickering seconds.
Let me see the peace that exists
In the eye of the storm.
Peace in the midst of activity.
Let me have that vision
In which questions and problems
Are lost in the vastness
Of the endless love
That surrounds me
This night and always.

FACING THE TRUTH

In this evening light
In my head
I can hear the words
Spoken today
Which hurt me.
They were unkind and probably meant to hurt.
My first reaction was to hit back
But when I think about it
Perhaps what hurt most
What made the remark sting
Was the element of truth in it.
And I suppose the fact is
I don't like being told the truth
About myself.

'Oh that God would give us
Eyes to see ourselves
As others see us.'
I would not really like that.
When I think about myself
I don't like to think about my failings.

I'm inclined to keep counting my qualities
To justify myself
To consider the flaws in my character
As minor blemishes.
The last thing I want
Is to see my faults
Nor do I want somebody else pointing at my sins.
So I am angry and hit back
Because the truth hurts.

Lord of the evening
In your presence
I can hide nothing.
You know me as I am
Inside and out.
Before you I am humbled
But not angry.
Why?
Is it because I know
That you will go on loving me
In spite of my weakness?

Lord, help me to listen
To criticism of myself
So that I might face the truth
And learn.
Help me to see the faults of my friends
With understanding,
To forgive,
And to go on loving
As you do.

A SMILE

Lord of the evening
There are some people
Who always make me feel better
For meeting them.
The people who make me smile.
They have a warmth about them, an inner gaiety.

After a few minutes in their company
The world seems a better place.
Somehow, my problems and difficulties
Are not nearly so bad.
What gift is it that such people have?
What is the secret of their infectious joy?

Lord I'm thinking about a particular friend
Who always makes me feel good.
Why is it that I am always lifted up
Simply by the presence of that friend?
I know that to give out warmth and joy
Is impossible without love.
Such a person has to have a loving, caring spirit.
Is it that they care more about people than things?
Is it that for the few minutes they are with me
I catch a glimpse of love at work?

Lord
Tomorrow I will meet a number of people
And I would like them to feel better
For having spent some time with me.
It will mean that I will have to think
More about them than myself
And that won't be easy,
It will take effort.
But of all the things
That I could spend my energy on
Few things could have more value
Than making someone smile
Or feel a little love.
Lord, help me to bring some joy or warmth
Into every meeting.

THE EMPTY HOUSE

Tonight I feel slightly lost,
Isolated, in need of company.
I always feel like this
When my family are away
Even for a few days.
My life feels empty
The house feels deserted
Just a house not a home.
The days seem to drag on
And I long for the return
Of voices, noise, laughter,
And I wonder how I would manage
If I was always alone.

Lord of the evening
Loneliness isn't just solitude
Or lack of company,
I have felt lonely
Even in the midst of my family
A deep aching void inside me,
Times when I have been unable to share
Worries, questions, guilt.
Times when my voice makes the right responses
My feet are firm on my own hearth-rug
But my mind is adrift,
Alone on a sea of anxieties.
Lord at these times
I seem to lose touch with my friends
And you.

In this particular evening reflection
I know that I am never really alone
But Lord, I need the assurance
That you are present with me
In my darkest moment,
That I do not have to seek you
Because you are always beside me.
Make your presence real for me
In all places and at all times
Pour your spirit
Of comfort and strength
Into every lonely mind, including mine.

Lord of the evening
Into your hands I commend my spirit.

I AM NOT WORTHY

This night
In your presence Lord
I lay the burden of my doubts
All unanswered questions
All the problems of my conscience
The wrongs that I have done to others
The guilt of things neglected;
The pain of cruel words
The stupidity of my pride and vanity
The arrogance and conceit of my selfishness
My little faith, my lack of love.

Lord I am not worthy to be in your presence
Say but the word and I shall be healed.

Lord this night
In your presence
I look for forgiveness,
I look for help.
Help me to love;
Help me to serve;
Help me to suffer;
Help me to trust;
Help me to live.
May your forgiving love
Live in me,
That it might no longer be I that live
But you who live in me.

The Lord said,
Come to me
All you that are heavy laden
And I will give you rest.

I will not leave you desolate.
I will come to you.

In that day you will know that I am in my father and you
in me, and I in you.

Lord, your love is too great
For me to understand.
Grant me a quiet night
And a perfect end.

COMFORT THE SORROWFUL

Lord of the evening
Today I received a letter
About a friend who has lost her husband.
She is distressed,
Confused, numbed
By grief.
Her world seems to have ended
And no-one feels able to help.
Nobody can reach her.

Her sorrow imprisons her
Like a stone wall.
Loving Lord
Show me how to help her.

So often I am embarrassed
By grief.
I don't know what to say
Or what to do;
And the easiest thing
Is to do nothing.
If I write it is so hard
To find the right words;
If I visit I feel at a loss
Uncomfortable
In the silence of sorrow.
Lord help me to make an attempt to comfort
Even if my efforts are stumbling
And inadequate.

Lord
Grief cannot be erased by magic.
But what would comfort me?
Perhaps the knowledge
That for the one I love
Suffering has ended.
I would like to be reminded
Of the promises of Chirst,
That he has gone
To prepare a place for us
So that where he is we shall be.

To be reminded that
The eye has not seen
Nor the ear heard
Nor has it entered the heart of man
What things have been prepared
For those that love God;
And that nothing
Can separate us from the love of Christ
Not even death.

Lord
In the presence of sorrow
Give me the courage
To share my faith.

MASKS

At the end of the day
I sometimes wonder if I have met anyone.
I mean *really* met.
Sometimes I think I have spent the day
Talking to images, façades, masks,
But never the person behind the eyes.

We all wear masks,
A different face for the boss
The bank manager
A friend.
I suppose masks
Can be good things,
Protective, reassuring,
But they do prevent meeting.
I know that if
I want to really meet someone,
I have to have the courage
To let my own mask fall.

If I am to know a friend,
My children,
Perhaps especially
If I am to know my wife,
We must be able to face each other
Without masks.

Lord of the night,
You know me
No matter what mask or façade
I may be showing to the world.
There is no way
That I can hide from you.
You know my weakness
And my strength
Better than I know myself.
Each day Lord,
Help me to be open and receptive
To those who need my friendship.
Help me not to hide
From those who need my love.
So that when I come before you
With nothing to conceal
What I am or what I have done,
I may dare to look
At the love in your face.

Lord of the evening, help me.

ALL MY TOMORROWS

Lord of the evening
The day has come to rest
And in the quiet, I am at peace.
I wish this calmness
Could stay with me
Throughout the working day.
Yet so often
I am irritable at the start of a day.
I wonder why?
I suppose there are physical reasons,
A natural reluctance
To leave the warmth and security
Of sleep;
And perhaps a deep-seated
Unwillingness to face the tasks
That await me.
Yet in any working day
The hours I spend with my family
Are so few
I can't afford to spoil any of them.

Lord
I know that when tomorrow begins
The things I say and do
Will create 'moods'
That will affect me and others
For hours.
One sharp word from me
Could mean that two or three
Other people will start
Off on the wrong foot.
It can make a difference
To so many things.

Lord
May I know the peace of your presence
When daylight breaks.
Tomorrow, help me to think before I speak
Help me to realise that I am not the only person
Who finds it difficult to start the day.
Let me know that your peace is present
Not only in the stillness of the night
But that in the midst
Of all the activities of the day.
I have only to breathe your name
To know your peace.
Help me to remember that
Now and always.

SONS AND DAUGHTERS

Tonight
I'm thinking about my children.
They're almost grown up now,
In their teens.
The eldest already has the vote
Is part of the electorate.
When I speak to one of my sons
On the telephone
I'm surprised to hear
A young man's voice.
Are these the children
Who squealed with delight
As we splashed at the sea-shore?
Who asked me
'Why did God make wasps?'
And
'Daddy, what was it like in the olden days?'

And now they are talking and thinking
About careers and jobs
Each with their secret hopes and dreams,
And it seems like only yesterday
That I stood in their place
And wondered about the future.
Yet *I* still have hopes and dreams
So what can I advise them?
That life is a continous exploration
An ongoing search for the dream,
That life is not a job or a qualification
Or a particular success,
But a series of discoveries.

Lord
How can I tell them
That even when they are pensioners
They will still be on the nursery slopes
Of discovery,
That the excitement of being alive
Is not arriving at destinations
Or achieving goals
But making the journey.
How can I convey to them
That they must never stop searching,
That if they do
They will have stopped living.

Lord help me in my life
To share with my children
The joy and the pain
Of the search.

I'M SORRY

I heard a man and a woman
Arguing in the street tonight.

Lord of the evening
Why is it so hard to say
I'm sorry?

Every day, homes are left in anger,
Front doors slammed,
Engines revved fiercely
Because of a few sharp, tetchy words,
Voices are raised about stupid, silly matters
And before we know where we are
People have parted.

Lord, it happens to me,
I don't want it to happen.

I don't ever want to leave in anger.
Even as the door shuts behind me
I ache with the stupidity of my own actions.
It takes just a few neurotic seconds
To create an atmosphere
That could take hours or years
To recover from.
It could all be over in seconds,
A quick hug, the words 'I'm sorry'.
But 'I'm sorry' is so hard to say.

Lord
Why is it so difficult
To make peace with each other?
No wonder there are wars.
Is it pride that holds my mouth tight,
A childish feeling
That I am not the one who should apologise?
It wasn't my fault?
In these flare-ups
What does it matter *whose* fault it is?
The only thing that matters is love and harmony.
Lord turning my back in anger is weakness,
It reduces me as a human being.
Give me the courage,
The stature,
To say, 'I'm sorry'.

. . . And may those two people
I heard in the street
End this day in mutual forgiveness.

EYES TO SEE

The setting sun is silent
Yet it tells its own story.
Before I see it again
That same sun will have shined
On vast continents,
Warmed rich and poor,
Made shadows on mountains,
Islands, jungles, cities.

And here I am
In the last of the day's light.
What can I see?
Just another day ended
Or thousands greeting a new day
In other lands?

In the waking light of my new day,
With toast and marmalade
And a cup of tea,
What will I see?
A hasty snack before the morning rush?
Or will there be on my table
Oranges from Spain,
Leaves from India,
Bread from the wheatfields
Of English Downs,
A humble breakfast or a feast?
Lord, give me eyes to see
In the light you shed upon the world.

Lord, let me see the magic
Of common place things.
Let me see the mystery of creation in the sky
That goes on being endless
Day after day.
Let me see the wonder of creation
In the families of birds
That have flown for thousands of years
Across endless miles of sea,
Guided by what?

Let me see the whole of creation
In a blade of grass
And the reason for it all
In an act of kindness.

Lord of the evening, open my eyes,
So that this night
Shall not be empty
But full of the knowledge of you.

A QUIET MIND

Tonight
I've had a curious thought,
It's a paradox,
The more I seek for a quiet mind
The more anxious I seem to become.
The more I examine my conscience
The more disturbed I become.
The more I try to plan the future
The more worried I become.
It's a simple rule really,
Anxiety breeds anxiety.

Lord, it cannot be wrong
To want a quiet mind
Or a bad thing to try
To clear my conscience.

And sometimes tomorrow
Has to be planned today.
Perhaps I try too hard,
Perhaps I do too much
Planning, and examining.
Perhaps I spend too much time
Thinking about the state I'm in,
Perhaps the real trouble
Is that I worry too much about me.

The times I have found peace
Are those times when
My mind has centred on something
Outside of myself,
Listening to somebody else's story,
Thinking about an idea in a book.
I have found contentment in physical work.
In fact on all those occasions
When I have been 'lost'
In something other than me.

Lord, this night
Help me to die to self,
So that I might awake
To live more fully
For others and in you.
Help me to trust
That as you have led me this far
Your guidance will continue.

THE CHILD AND THE FATHER

Lord of the evening
Here I am again
Like a child
Who needs comfort and reassurance.
Lord, I keep coming to you
With regrets.
I keep asking you to do things for me.
As a parent I know that I cannot always
Do everything for my children,
I know that they have to stand
On their own feet.
Perhaps the best thing
That I can offer my children
Is the love that assures them
That no matter what happens
They can always come home.

Right now I need the assurance
Of that kind of love,
That you will be standing by me
When things go right
And when things go wrong.
I often wonder if my children
Believe me.
I wonder if they ever feel
That some problem simply
Cannot be shared with me,
I wonder if they really trust me.
Trusting is difficult,
Yet without trust
There can be no peace of mind.

Lord in the days that lie before me
Help me to trust in your loving presence;
In the knowledge
That at the end of every day
I can come to you
As a child to a father.

Lord of the evening,
Heavenly Father,
Hear my prayer.

COURAGE FOR THE NIGHT

Lord of the evening
The day has passed
But the day's problems are still with me.
Sometimes I wish the day away,
I long for the night,
Hoping that sleep
Will envelop my difficulties,
Banish them forever
Beneath the blanket of darkness;
That I might rise to a fresh, new day
With my slate wiped clean.
But day follows day
And I am still the same person
With the same problems, questions, difficulties.

Lord, I wish I could stand at a distance,
Far away from today,
Then perhaps I could smile
At today's problems.
If I look at last year's worries
Or even last month's
I know for a fact that I survived,
And that gives me hope.
But I don't want to run away
Or live my life at a distance,
I want to enjoy
The daily battle of life
As I live it.

Tonight Lord,
Give me courage
To see tomorrow as a friend,
As a new opportunity to put things right,
To see the new day as a gift,
My millionth chance to start again,
To see that the new day
Is rich in possibilities,
That even the wildest dreams
Can come true
Where there is faith, hope and love.

Lord, fill my dreams tonight
With your spirit
So that I might face the world
Armed with these gifts
That nothing can destroy.

THE HOPE OF HIS COMING

Here I wait in quiet hope
That you will come
To water my barren fields,
To make blossom the flower and fruit
That wither in merciless heat.
Do not forsake me.

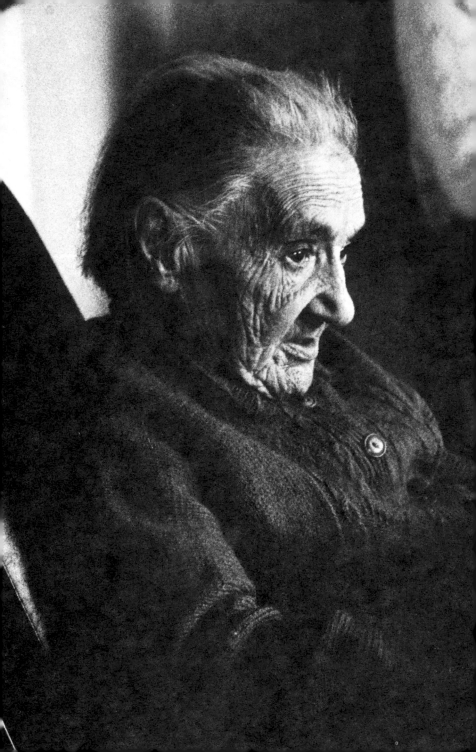

I am the earth
On which large eyed children thirst and die.
I am the crusted soil
Watered by the tears
Of mothers, fathers, sons and daughters.
Hear my cry,
Father, I thirst.

Here I wait in quiet hope
That you will come
To open the door to release me,
For I am a prisoner.
Here I sit, in many places,
In prisons political and criminal.
In labour camp, in hospital,
In the high-rise flat,
In a bed-sitting room.
Imprisoned by my brother.
Hear me when I call,
And come to me.
Now is the time of your coming
Do not pass me by.

Here I wait in quiet hope
That you will come
To possess my being,
To inhabit me,
For I have no strength left,
No power to lift myself,
Every sinew, every bone
Fast bound by selfishness,

Grasping at life
There is nothing my hands can hold
Nothing preserve.
I can struggle no more,
Defeated, defenceless, exhausted.
So Lord,
Here I wait in quiet hope
That you will come.

Save us Lord, while we are awake;
Protect us while we sleep;
That we may keep watch with Christ
And rest with him in peace.

BEFORE I SLEEP

Lord, before I sleep
Help me to share with you
The things I am anxious about,
For I am anxious about many things;
About my family,
About relationships with people,
About the future.
I am anxious about security;
Money in the bank,
A pension, income-tax returns,
Rates, a roof over our heads,
Clothes on our backs,
Food in the larder.

And the Lord said,
Be not anxious about your life, what you shall eat, nor

about your body, what you shall wear, for life is more than food and the body more than clothing. Which of you by being anxious can add a cubit to his span of life? Your father knows that you need these things. Instead seek his Kingdom and all these things shall be yours as well.

Lord, before I sleep
Help me to remember with gratitude
All the blessings of my life;
For the home into which I was born,
For the friends that I grew up with
In school and afterwards,
Help me to be grateful for companionship,
For laughter, and family love.
Help me to be worthy of your trust,
To be grateful for the people
You have given me to love.
For your endless grace to me,
For in seeing your goodness
I am lifed above the troubles of the day-to-day.
Give me a grateful mind,
A mind aware of the love that is poured out,
Given freely,
Even to the least deserving.

And the Lord said through his apostle Paul,
*Let your requests be made known to God;
And the peace of God
Which passes all understanding
Will keep your heart and mind in Christ.*

Lord, before I sleep
Help me to see
What is important and what is not.
Show me the secret
That enabled Paul to be content
In any situation.
Help me to give into your care,
My life, my talents, my time.
Help me to know the strength and peace
That comes to those
Who totally submit their lives
To Christ.
In spite of my failings,
My self-will, my arrogance,
My pride, my ambitions.
Take my life Lord, in spite of me,
In spite of my own self-deceit.
Take my life and let it be
Consecrated, Lord, to thee.

Father,
The moment I lift my eyes towards you
I move from the darkness of self
Into the light of your love.
The brightness
Of your goodness and love
Melts away anxieties,
Like morning sun on the mist of night.
The warmth of that light upon my brow
Brings, beyond understanding,
Peace, like summer sun.

And the breeze on my face
Is the kiss of your spirit.

Lord,
Help me to be quiet and still
In the peace of your presence
This night and always.

CHRISTMAS EVE

On this special night,
I am thinking about children.
Since the day began
Thousands of children have been born,
In hospitals, homes, shanty towns,
Children who have opened their eyes
For the first time.
Even at this moment,
Somewhere, a child
Is drawing its first breath in total innocence.
There is something of a mystery about babies,
Especially at Christmas time.

A child,
Wide, open-eyed trusting infant
Who draws love from me, and returns it.
There is hope in the *fact*
Of the newly born;
So much potential for love.
When I look at a baby
Who holds my finger
In a tiny gentle grip,
I find it hard to imagine
That I was once a child.

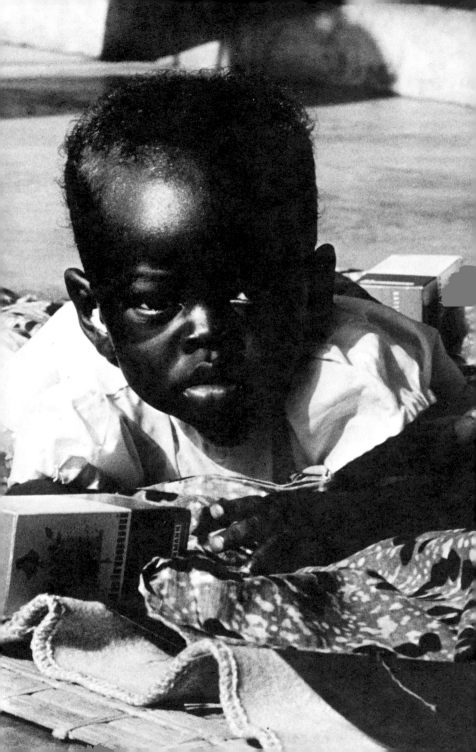

Did I have so much potential for love?
What happened to that child
That made hardness, suspicion,
Envy and malice, grow?
Did simplicity have to die?

Soon on Christmas Day,
People will sing and rejoice,
Children will laugh and play
In celebration of the birth of a child
Whose name became love.

Lord of this special night
Help me to protect innocence
Wherever I see it.
Help me not to abuse the simplicity of children
Who look to me to learn.
Help me to nurture love and truth;
And let the love and truth
That was born in a stable so long ago,
Be born again in me tonight.

THE INSTRUMENTS OF PEACE

This meditation was written when the author was a university chaplain. It was later broadcast in the BBC programme 'Lighten our Darkness'.

Cold and shivering we stood
Around the Ditchling Beacon,
High on Sussex Downs,
Sussex students and chaplain
Not much older,
Sipping soup from steaming flasks
As rosey girls unpacked sandwiches
And waited for the dawn.

In the first light
We gave thanks for the night long trek
With the singing of the hymn,
Dear Lord and Father of Mankind
Forgive our Foolish Ways.
We sang and rubbed our itching eyes.
No one saw the flight begin
But there, in the centre of our circle,
A lark had risen, as if from the midst of us;
And soaring higher and higher
Surprised us with his voice.

A tiny bird bursting with song
That filled our eyes with joy,
Our ears with his thrill
And printed on our memories
A moment of peace
That soothes me still.
And so we sang,

Drop thy still dews of quietness
Till all our strivings cease;
Take from our souls the strain and stress
And let our ordered lives confess
The beauty of thy peace.

Strivings, strain and stress
All too readily rule my frame;
The petty worries of every day,
Work and years sometimes seem
To press upon my brain.
While deep inside my inner pit,
Inadequacy and anxiety
Howl like hounds
Whose appetites feed on fret,
And yet,
The instruments of thy peace
Are all around me;
Not a feast of exquisite song
From a bird on a lonely heath,
But instruments more mundane
Like photographs and smiles
And cups of tea and the leaves
Of busy lizzies in plastic flower pots.

Your song sings in the sound of water
Running from a tap,
From down at heel pigeons
Cooing in the eaves,
Kettles boiling, winds whistling
Or waves breaking endlessly on a beach;.
These are friends,
These laughing, talking, smiling
Instruments of thy peace.

There are friends
I never speak to
Because they live
In books and plays.
Performers on the television
Who in their myriad ways speak to me.
They are not the least
Of the instruments of thy peace.

Love surrounds me most in people,
Like those friends who are the healers, comforters,
The laughter makers who walk into my life,
Through my office, or through my kitchen door.
But those I love most
Who give me most
Are so very close that I am apt to ignore,
To miss, the kiss of peace they bring.
Yet when I emerge from under my shell
I am lifted, helped, dazzled by the love
Which is the wonder of the music
Of the instrument of peace.

Lord, I want to be
An instrument of your peace.
I sometimes wish I could do
Heroic things; be a saint;
Do something beautiful for you.
But there is nothing extraordinary about me.
I gaze at the great saints with awe
And their very saintliness is frightening.

Yet in my own experience
The instruments of your peace
Have never been very dramatic.
Your peace has come to me
Through simple, common things,
Acts of kindness,
Gestures of love from people
Who have accidentally given me a glimpse
Of your love.
But perhaps I can only bear to see a glimpse
Of the love that embraces the world,
The love that laughs, weeps, lives and dies
With and for the whole of humanity.
Perhaps a glimpse is all I can take.

Lord, let me reflect the light
That *is* given to me,
Let me recognise the love and the joy
And the peace that *is* in my life
And to share it,
With whoever will receive it.

Help me to be an instrument of your peace
In the very ordinary acts of my day,
From my rising to my sleeping,
In talking, in listening, in patience,
In caring, in laughing, in thinking.

Lord make me an instrument of thy peace,
Where there is hatred let me sow love;
Where there is injury, pardon;
Where there is discord, union;
Where there is doubt, faith;
Where there is despair, hope;
Where there is darkness, light;
Where there is sadness, joy;
For thy mercy's sake.
Amen.

THE LANGUAGE OF PRAYER

To explore the depths of human love takes a long time, a lifetime, or longer. To search the mystery of divine love takes eternity and that, poets say, is far too short. Left to my own devices I would have wasted so much time. Years and years could have been spent in a spiritual wilderness if it hadn't been for one thing, one thing that was right out of my control.

In infancy, before I could speak, I heard a particular language. As water was sprinkled on my head, I was received into the family of Christ. The precious sign of the cross was traced on my brow. Before I could speak, I was asked to walk with God all the days of my life. As others answered for me I heard the language of love, without understanding I heard my parents pray.

As I learned to speak, so I learned prayers, prayers that would never leave me. I didn't consciously learn them, I just heard them so often that I knew them; the Lord's Prayer, Glory Be To God, Hail Mary. I did memorise the mysteries of the rosary and learn the prayers of the mass because I wanted to be involved in the drama and mystery of candles and incense. I sang 'Kyries', listened with awe to the whispered words, 'Hoc est corpus meum', 'this is my body'; attended 'Benediction' and 'Holy Hour' services; was confirmed, made my first confession and communion; followed the stations of the cross; made 'Novenas' and grew into a scuffed-shoed, cut-kneed, scruffy lad who had heard the language of prayer, but through a glass, very darkly.

In those days prayer came as naturally as breathing. In retrospect they were happy days, mostly. Of course at the time they seemed to be full of the disasters and pains of growing up, but God was as real as my parents and my brothers. He was one of the family, unquestioned.

I used to play in a parish band in which my family were well represented, my father, my uncle and my cousins amounting to two trombones, two cornets and a tenor horn. It's odd, but there is a particular piece of music, 'Panis Angelicus', which whenever I hear it, I see my uncle with his trombone and the memory of the quality of those days comes flooding back.

Slowly, as it does for most of us, childhood began to disappear, and with it the ease of natural prayer. Questions began to push prayer into the background and soon the questions became all important.

I remember plucking up the courage to visit a priest, to present my questions to him. They worried me, these questions, I probably thought that nobody had ever asked them before. They were questions about the church.

I was playing my first semantic game of 'what does the church mean when she says ...?' and out came the questions about the real presence, transubstantiation, Aristotle's theories about accidents and substance. I thought I was no end of a budding theologian. I remember the priest listening patiently, and then saying in his gentle Irish brogue, 'you know, the trouble with you is pride, intellectual pride, it's the devil making you ask these questions, the devil in the form of intellectual pride'. So I said to the priest, 'well, if it is the devil asking these questions, what do you say to the devil?' The priest smiled and said, 'get thee behind me Satan'.

I went off in a dissatisfied huff, but of course he was right, it was pride that was separating me from God. It took me a long time to realise that truth. It was very much later that I realised that I had fallen out with particular teachings of the church, but had never asked the basic questions, such as, 'Do I believe in God? Do I believe in Jesus?' Sadly I slid into a cynical agnosticism which lasted for several years.

I remember feeling slightly ashamed as a teenager in the forces abroad, in a moment of stress and fear I found myself saying 'Hail Mary . . .' I felt ashamed because I had let my principles go and resorted to prayer through fear. I also felt ashamed that when I tried to pray the only words that I could form were those I had learned as a child, and in this situation they were not particularly appropriate. I felt ashamed because I didn't know how else to pray. It took several more years before I could turn to God and say simply, 'I don't know how to pray, but please come into my life, somehow'.

In time and through various experiences, I began to realise, that I had turned my back on God, but he had never left me. He was still as close as he was when I was a child. I wanted to start again, but it's not simple. The easy, natural acceptance had gone with childhood and innocence. The old priest was right, my intellect kept getting in the way, pride and doubt had become part of me.

It was at the least expected moment that I realised the presence of God. In the middle of an argument, when my cynicism was working at its hardest. Suddenly all the clever words, the doubts, just dropped away, like someone opening a curtain, for a brief moment, the arguments fell away before what was to me a moment of reality.

Since then I have discovered that there is no one way of praying. I have talked with God using the beautiful ancient prayers of the church, using my own stumbling words, and sometimes using no words.

Sometimes I hear a piece of music as a shout of praise. Sometimes I pray the news, just listen to the headlines and offer up the concerns of the day, the world. Sometimes I let the world shut God out again and it is a struggle to realise his presence. I find silence is often the best way back. The silence of a church, or inner silence that can be found sitting in a rush-hour train. Simply to sit quietly, not asking questions, not listing my problems, not saying anything, simply being still in his presence. It is in these moments when God lifts the curtain to reveal that most of the perils, changes and fears of my life come from within.

I sometimes go into retreat, perhaps for a week in some quiet house. I also go into retreat for much shorter periods. By that I mean, not weeks or days or hours, but seconds. In the middle of an ordinary day, I will close my eyes for a few seconds and in those seconds retreat to a place where I have known both the peace and the presence of God. Anyone can do it. We all know of such places and in the twinkling of an eye we can be there. For me there is a particular bay of an island in the Hebrides, which has a rock which we christened 'Oyster-catcher Island'. I have only to close my eyes and I am there, breathing in the beauty and the calm of one of God's great works of art.

That crag of rock
Whose head stands proud where shell and tide
Have formed a face;
Granite jowled and limpet eyed,
That watches cloud and rain-filled sky
And hears the piercing, plaintive cry
Of gull and oyster-catcher.

That rock
The children climbed, shouting,
With breathless counting of the steps
By which they timed the speed of their ascent.
That rock
Heather crowned and bird bespattered,
Stands in seaweed daily drowned by flooding seas
That break about its feet.

And still it stands
Serene with ancient calm,
Aloof, impassive
Unmoved by tears, untouched by grief
Of those whose fretful years are far too brief
For this eternal stone.

That ageless rock
Calls in its silence across the noisy clamour
Of the city,
And the passing drama of men struggling
For a short-lived space of comfort or power
Or a transitory place in the sun of our
Particular day.

The warlords and the captains
Took sightings from this tor
And dropped their sails to anchor in its lee.
But now, children's cries and breaker's roar
Join the endless washing of the sea
Above the buried bones and swords
Of yesterday's strife.

That rock
That feels the lap of silken smooth serenity
Yet hears the scream
And roar of a tempest sea
In all its agony.
That rock
Seen between the mists of heather blue,
Seems to know the sorrow and elation
Of the mind in whose creation
The sculptured souls of men
Are washed in a sea of love
And gathered into eternity.

And though my feet
Tread city's stone
And ears are tuned to thousands teeming,
Yet mind and heart still stand alone
By sea and rock forever dreaming
Of that endless day.

If it takes eternity to search out the mystery of divine love, then I have a long way to go before I even begin to fathom the depths, but this far I have come. I know that if I can be still, in my head, even for a few seconds, he will enter my mind, bring light where there is darkness, replace anxiety with his peace. In such brief moments of stillness, I am a child again. In such brief moments, I am deep in prayer.